news™

SUICIDE BOMBERS

Robert Greenberger

ROSEN
PUBLISHING®

New York

For Kate, who is striving to help make the world a safer place

Published in 2007 by The Rosen Publishing Group, Inc.
29 East 21st Street, New York, NY 10010

Library of Congress Cataloging-in-Publication Data

Greenberger, Robert.
Suicide bombers / Robert Greenberger.—1st ed.
    p. cm.—(In the news)
Includes bibliographical references and index.
ISBN-13: 978-1-4042-0977-0
ISBN-10: 1-4042-0977-8 (library binding)
1. Terrorism—Juvenile literature. 2. Suicide bombers—Juvenile literature. 3. Suicide bombings—Juvenile literature. I. Title.
HV6431.G7263 2007
363.325—dc22

                                                    2006023528

Manufactured in the United States of America

On the cover: Top, above: An English Muslim woman protests the July 14, 2005, London bombings by Islamic terrorists. Top, below: Islamic Jihad supporters dressed as suicide bombers stage an anti-Israel protest. Bottom, left: A girl holds up a picture of herself and her dead brother, killed in a Baghdad suicide bombing. Bottom, right: U.S. soldiers patrol the site of a restaurant destroyed in a Baghdad suicide bombing.

contents

1

A Brief History of Suicide Terrorism

S ince the beginning of the new millennium, it seems that hardly a week goes by without the news reporting another suicide bomb attack somewhere in the world. Attacks by Palestinians in Israel are common. Sunni Muslims killed dozens of Shiite Muslims and American soldiers in Iraq on an almost daily basis in 2005 and the first half of 2006 during the American occupation of that country. Devastating suicide terror attacks by Islamist radicals on public transportation systems in Spain in 2004 and England in

2005 killed hundreds of people. The most dramatic and deadly suicide attack in history occurred on American shores on September 11, 2001, when four hijacked commercial jets were used to attack the World Trade Center in New York City and the Pentagon in Arlington, Virginia.

Smoke rises following a suicide bombing attack in Baghdad, Iraq, on September 14, 2005.

To people living in North America, the reasons behind why people would end their lives in such a grisly, murderous fashion are often incomprehensible. However, people have been using suicide attacks to wage a war or stage an extreme form of political protest for thousands of years.

The term "suicide attacker" was first used in the 1940s, during World War II. The *New York Times* first used the term "suicide bomber" on August 10, 1940, when describing a German military strategy, and the phrase entered the lexicon. It quickly became more often associated with Japanese kamikaze pilots, who would fly their planes directly into Allied warships in order to sink them.

It wasn't until the 1980s, however, that the term became commonly used, coinciding with the rise in suicide attacks in the Middle East. Muslims often refer to an attacker as a *shahid* (or "bomber"). The terrorist organizations that recruit, train, and send attackers out call them "martyrdom operatives," meaning they are giving their lives for a holy cause (usually the destruction of Israel and the liberation of Palestinians, or a more general Islamist strike against the "infidels" of the West).

This book will explore the long history of suicide attacks, their modern development, what turns people toward such extreme acts of violence, and their effectiveness as either political protest or combat tactic.

Suicide as Symbolic Protest

Historically, certain groups of people have often felt oppressed or mistreated by those who control the wealth and power in society or who are of a ruling political or ethnic class. When a group of people feel they have been pushed to a point where they can no longer abide the harsh, unjust, or discriminatory conditions in which they are forced to live, they tend to fight back. In almost every case, the rebellion, revolt, or uprising involves some level of violence. Often the rebellious group is outmatched by better-armed and better-trained forces.

Sometimes the ragtag group seeking political change or government overthrow is so poorly equipped or outnumbered that they resort to largely symbolic acts of protest rather than full-scale, direct military engagement of government forces. These activities can range from graffiti and marches to more serious acts of vandalism, sabotage, and self-violence.

Self-violence is a relatively rare but powerful form of political protest. Self-immolation (burning oneself to death) and hunger strikes, for example, have been used throughout history to draw attention to a cause, make a dramatic point, and shame and embarrass the ruling government. In the twen-

A woman pays her respects before a memorial dedicated to Bobby Sands, an Irish political prisoner who died in a British prison during a hunger strike in 1981.

tieth century, these extreme tactics have been used to protest the Vietnam War, British treatment of Irish political prisoners, and U.S. detention of suspected Islamist radicals at the Guantanamo Bay Naval Base in Cuba. Unlike suicide attacks—in which someone resolves to kill him- or herself while taking as many other people with him or her as possible—these actions take only the life of the protester, not of any innocent victims.

Rebel organizations can also resort to small-scale actions that, in addition to making a symbolic statement,

A Buddhist monk commits ritual suicide by lighting himself on fire in the central market square of Saigon in 1963. He was protesting the South Vietnamese government's anti-Buddhist policies.

direct a very real violence outward into the general population, inflicting devastation and taking many lives. In many people's minds, terrorist activities—including suicide attacks—undermine whatever moral authority the oppressed or rebellious group may have originally possessed. Sheikh Ahmed Yassin, leader of the Palestinian terrorist group Hamas, justifies the tactic of suicide bombing by saying, "Once we have warplanes and missiles, then we can think of changing our means of legitimate self-defense. But right now, we can only tackle the fire with our bare hands and sacrifice ourselves" (as quoted in Mia Bloom's book *Dying to Kill*).

The Kamikaze Pilots of World War II

The twentieth century's first major introduction to suicide attacks were the Japanese kamikaze pilots of World War II. Japanese culture had long endorsed the idea of honorable suicide—known as *seppuku*—and suicide attacks were considered a proper way to engage the enemy. Thousands of Japanese warplanes were intentionally flown directly into U.S. warships, sinking or damaging about 350 of them and killing or wounding more than 10,000 American servicemen. About 3,000 Japanese pilots died during these attacks, which wreaked havoc, destruction, and mass death. The word "kamikaze" translates as "divine wind" and is thought to refer to a thirteenth-century typhoon that saved Japan from Mongol invaders.

Professor Yuki Tanaka of the Hiroshima Peace Institute wrote about the motivations of the kamikaze pilots. He identified five sentiments that inspired the majority of them:

1. Rationalizing one's own death to defend one's country and its people.

2. The belief that to die for one's country was to show duty and respect for one's own parents, particularly for one's mother.
3. Strong solidarity with their flight mates who shared their fate as kamikaze pilots.
4. Strong sense of responsibility and contempt for cowardice.
5. A lack of a clear, humanized image of the enemy.

The last item is most telling, indicating the level of philosophical indoctrination and emotional separation the pilots underwent in the years prior to and during the war.

With the Allied victory in Europe against the forces of Germany—Japan's fellow Axis ally—World War II began winding down, and Japanese military leaders knew they were destined to lose. As a military tactic, suicide flights were of limited success, considering the loss of pilots and the expense of building replacement aircraft.

In addition to the better-known kamikaze air attacks, the Japanese also employed modified, manned torpedoes called *kaiten*. These two-man submarine missiles initially were built with escape hatches. In later models, however, these hatches were removed once it became clear that no naval crew would be coming back from their missions. The bomb-laden kaiten was aimed at a target, and just before impact, the soldiers manning it would embrace and then shoot one another in the head.

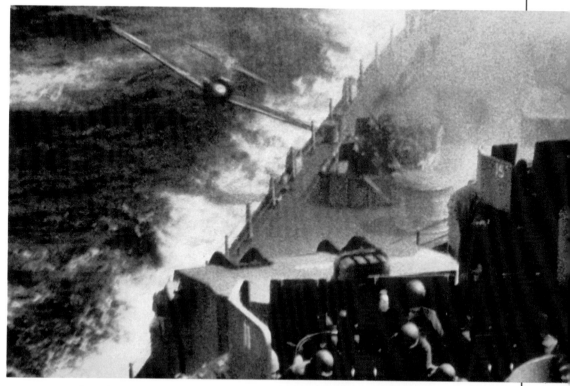

A Japanese kamikaze pilot prepares to crash his plane into the side of a U.S. Pacific Fleet warship in 1945 during World War II.

The Japanese were not the only Axis power to engage in such desperate warfare. As Germany got overwhelmed by the Allied forces in Europe, orders were given for their Rammjager aircraft to take out enemy bombers. These reinforced airplanes allowed pilots to bail out. As the war wore down, however, the command insisted that pilots go down with their planes. Pilots for these suicide missions were initially volunteers, but eventually servicemen who violated the German code of conduct were forced to fly the aircraft.

The Emergence of Suicide Bombers in the Middle East

Although historians may disagree on the exact incident that began the current cycle of suicide attacks, all agree that it occurred in the Middle East. For centuries, that region of the world has been beset with political, religious, and territorial disputes that have frequently led to bloodshed, war, and countless fatalities.

Lebanon

Lebanon is most often cited as the location where the first modern-day suicide bomber struck. In December 1981, the country was embroiled in a civil war among various Christian, Muslim, and Palestinian political factions and their armed militias, when the Dawa Party—a Shiite Muslim fundamentalist group devoted to ending Christian rule of Lebanon and resisting Western influences—exploded a car bomb in front of the Iraqi Embassy in Beirut. It had the desired effect of shocking the citizens, and the world at large, so it was repeated with increasing frequency and efficiency.

In 1982, Israel invaded and occupied southern Lebanon with 17,000 soldiers in order to prevent cross-border attacks against it by Islamist radicals. Hezbollah, a militant Islamic organization dedicated to ending the Israeli occupation, was formed in July of that year. In April 1983, the United States Embassy in Beirut was attacked by a suicide bomber driving a delivery van packed with explosives.

The following October, the French and American barracks of a multinational force serving in Lebanon were attacked by a suicide truck bomber, killing 241 U.S. Marines and 58 French paratroopers. Most Western countries, including the United States, blamed both attacks on Hezbollah and labeled it a terrorist organization. The group continues to deny responsibility, and the link has never been definitively proven. Regardless, Hezbollah had become the target of international condemnation.

Five months later, U.S. troops left Lebanon, and Hezbollah celebrated the effectiveness of the attacks,

British soldiers help evacuate a wounded U.S. Marine following the Hezbollah suicide truck bombing of the U.S. Marine command center near the Beirut airport in Lebanon on October 23, 1983.

despite denying credit for them. This only fueled the interest of other radical organizations in using suicide bombings as a terrorist tactic. The troop withdrawal seemed to lend credibility to the suicide attack's effectiveness as a political and military tool for small, poorly armed radical groups to get their way.

Hezbollah crossed international borders on March 17, 1992, when a suicide car bomber attacked the Israeli Embassy in Buenos Aires, Argentina, killing 29 and wounding 242. The group that claimed credit for this was

Islamic Jihad, but it stated that the attack was in retaliation for Israel's assassination of Hezbollah leader Sheikh Abbas al-Musawi, his wife, and their child one month earlier in southern Lebanon. Israel finally left Lebanon in 2000 (though it re-entered southern Lebanon in the summer of 2006). But it never cited the more than fifty suicide attacks targeted against its institutions and citizens by Lebanese-based terrorists as a factor in the decision.

Palestine

Though suicide bombing emerged in Lebanon in the early 1980s, it was not until 1991 that Palestinian terrorists first resorted to suicide bombings in their war against Israel and its occupation of territory claimed by Palestinians. The conflict between Israel and Palestine dates back to biblical times, as both cultures claim much of the same territory as their exclusive holy land. But it was the creation of the Israeli nation in 1948 that began to spur the Palestinian people into action.

The modern state of Israel was founded on land that had been occupied by various groups of people, including Palestinians. The Palestinians disliked the land they were assigned in order to make room for Israel and the fact that they were not allowed to form their own state. As a result, they refused to recognize Israel's nationhood and its very right to exist.

Two members of a Jewish defense force exchange gunfire with Arab militants in Tel Aviv in 1947.

As Israel struggled for survival in the succeeding decades while surrounded by hostile Arab neighbors, the Palestinian people—living as refugees in surrounding Arab countries, particularly Lebanon—lost more and more of their traditional lands as a result of failed Arab military conflicts with Israel, most notably the Six Days' War of 1967. Each time Israel beat back attacks by its Arab neighbors, it annexed more land in order to create a safe buffer between it and the armies of the various enemy nations around it. The Oslo Accords of 1993 offered Palestinians, in exchange for finally recognizing Israeli statehood, autonomy in parts of the West Bank and Gaza, two important territories long claimed by Palestinians and lost in 1967.

Since then, the Palestinian people, initially led by Yasir Arafat (1929–2004) and his Palestine Liberation Organization (PLO), have struggled to gain statehood on their own terms. Unfortunately, the people were splintered into several different factions, each with its own extreme view on how to resolve the Israel-Palestine problem. In addition to Arafat's Fatah party, one of the

During a 2004 anti-Israel rally in the Gaza Strip, Hamas supporters wear mock explosive belts, similar to those worn by suicide bombers.

most successful of these political factions has been Hamas, which wages the battle for Palestinian statehood on two fronts. The first is the winning of the hearts and minds of the Palestinian people by serving as a social services organization in an impoverished refugee society that has very few public services. Hamas keeps the streets clean, sets up and runs schools, and provides money and health care to the poor. The second front of its battle is considerably less positive—an unrelenting series of violent terrorist attacks on the Israeli people and their settlements—many of them suicide bombs in

Palestinian women line up to receive financial aid from a charity operated by Hamas.

restaurants and marketplaces and on public buses.

The Palestine Liberation Organization and its political wing Fatah (which represented the majority of Palestinians from the 1970s through the 1990s), along with Hamas and other Palestinian splinter groups, have appealed to either people's sense of historical and national outrage or their spirituality, or both, in order to inspire them to join their cause. While the PLO is secular (nonreligious), Hamas, Hezbollah, and Palestinian Islamic Jihad—all deemed to be terrorist groups by Western nations—invoke God's name when recruiting for membership and for terrorist attacks. They offer the people a specific interpretation of the Koran (the Islamic holy book) that allows them to commit both suicide and murder for the purposes of fighting nonbelievers, despite the fact that most Islamic scholars believe the Koran expressly forbids both acts. The ultimate goal of these terrorist groups is to create an Islamic holy land—including all of the land currently occupied by Israel—that would welcome all followers of Islam from around the world.

The Palestinian use of the suicide bomber originally grew in reaction to specific events starting on October 9, 1990, when Islamic followers left the al-Aqsa Mosque in Jerusalem and immediately began throwing stones at Jews praying at the Wailing Wall. Israeli police fired their guns to protect the unarmed Israeli worshippers, killing eighteen Palestinians as the day wore on. As a result, Hamas invoked a jihad, or "holy war." Omar abu Sirhan was the first to respond to the call, armed only with a butcher's knife. He managed to kill three people, fully expecting to die in the process. Instead, he was captured and became a Hamas hero. After this call to jihad, conflict with Israel involved coordinated terrorist attacks, often featuring suicide bombers.

On April 16, 1991, twenty-two-year-old Sahar Tamam Nabulsi, a member of Hamas, drove a van filled with cooking-gas canisters into two buses, wounding eight Israelis and killing a fellow Palestinian. In the following decade, according to *Time* magazine, there were 105 other suicide attacks, killing an additional 339 people.

The Palestinians call these kinds of suicidal missions "no escape" attacks, since there is no chance that the attacker will survive these planned raids on buildings and people. While the "no escape" incidents have occurred in the occupied Palestinian territories, the suicide bombers have mostly struck within Israel's pre-1967 borders, thereby reducing the risk of accidentally killing fellow Palestinians.

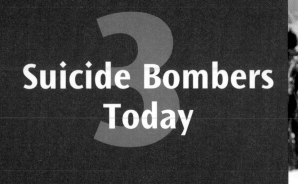

Suicide Bombers Today

In Afghanistan throughout the 1990s, an Islamic extremist group known as the Taliban ruled the country with an iron hand. Anything that deviated from the ruling clerics' Islamic fundamentalist view of life was outlawed, confiscated, or destroyed, and those who broke the religious law were frequently killed.

An important ally of the fundamentalist leadership was Osama bin Laden, who, with the Taliban's blessing and support, directed the terrorist activities of the organization known as Al Qaeda from within Afghanistan's borders.

He funded this group with his share of his Saudi Arabian family's oil-derived wealth. Al Qaeda has sponsored international terrorist activities in the hopes of spreading bin Laden's vision of reclaiming all lands once held by Muslims around the world and uniting all believers in a single, powerful Islamic state. A series of small-scale suicide attacks against Western interests throughout the 1990s gave no hint of the massive destruction that was about to be unleashed.

Osama bin Laden, Al Qaeda, and 9/11

Osama bin Laden has recruited, trained, and directed a global network of followers, spreading not only his fundamentalist beliefs but also his brand of terror. To him, suicide bombings are an effective and powerful symbolic statement, saying, in effect, that the Islamic martyrs are purer and more committed than those they destroy with their bombs. Each suicide bombing also seems to offer a troubling, threatening promise that others will surely follow.

A series of small-scale Al Qaeda suicide attacks against Western interests throughout the 1990s gave no hint of the massive destruction that was about to be unleashed.

Bin Laden went from a distant threat and relatively minor irritant to public enemy number one on September 11, 2001, when nineteen of his followers hijacked four

21

CNN EXCLUSIVE

Terrorist mastermind and leader of Al Qaeda Osama bin Laden strolls with masked and armed bodyguards in a secret location in Afghanistan in 2002.

American airplanes and essentially transformed the fuel-filled jets into massive suicide bombs. Two of the planes were diverted from their courses and flown directly into New York City's World Trade Center. The twin towers collapsed, killing thousands. A third plane was aimed at the Pentagon in Arlington, Virginia, just outside Washington, D.C., killing 189 people. The fourth plane crashed in a Pennsylvania field after passengers fought back, possibly preventing the White House or the Capitol from being attacked. The official death toll of the entire series of hijackings and subsequent attacks was set at 2,986.

Bin Laden proved that with careful planning and patience, the largest suicide bomb attack in history could be successfully executed. The cost of the entire operation was calculated to be about $100,000, a relatively modest amount that other terrorist groups could easily raise.

The countries victimized by Al Qaeda and like-minded terrorist organizations did not sit still. America and allied nations sent their armed forces into Afghanistan, throwing the Taliban from power and sending bin Laden and his close circle of advisers into hiding. Soon thereafter, in March 2003, the United States changed its focus to the terrorist threat the administration of President George W. Bush claimed was festering in Iraq, led by the dictator Saddam Hussein.

Iraq

The United States was determined to drive Saddam Hussein, long a thorn in America's side, out of power once and for all. One of the Bush administration's major justifications for going to war with Hussein, in addition to the alleged terror threat, was the eventually discredited claim that Iraq possessed weapons of mass destruction hidden throughout the country. Hussein had demonstrated his volatility many times before, and the American public worried that he might attack Israel or provide terrorists intent on striking the United States with chemical, biological, or even nuclear weapons.

Another major justification for the war put forth by the Bush administration and its coalition partners was their stated desire to free the Iraqi people from tyranny and bring democracy to the Middle East. The American public was told that, after toppling Hussein, U.S. armed forces would be welcomed as heroes and liberators by the Iraqi people. However, military strategists in Washington, D.C., did not accurately anticipate the level of resistance among several factions of Iraqis that occurred in the wake of the invasion, particularly among the Sunni Muslims who had supported Hussein. Iraq quickly became a magnet for Islamic freedom fighters who wanted to end the U.S. occupation of a Muslim nation and prevent America from establishing any true influence in the region.

Journalist Zaki Chehab recounts in his book *Inside the Resistance* how he accompanied a ragtag group of Iraqis in the city of Mosul who were resisting the American invasion.

They consisted of former army officers, former Baathists [members of Saddam Hussein's political party], members of Fedayeen Saddam, or affiliated to one of the Islamic organizations. They were united by the single objective of protecting their city against the American occupation. For them,

Saddam Hussein was still the president, and they would continue his work. One of them told me, "We are prepared to sacrifice out lives just as Hamas and its military wing in Palestine have done, and this can be repeated not just in Mosul but all over Iraq" . . . This was the first hint that suicide bombings would become a feature of this war of resistance.

An Iraqi fireman collects human remains following the suicide bombing of a mosque in Baghdad, Iraq, in 2006.

The insurgency planned these suicide bombings to occur in three steps, against three distinct targets. First, American soldiers would be attacked. Next to be targeted would be members of the international coalition supporting the American troops. Third, Iraqis viewed as collaborators—those who were aiding either the coalition forces, those joining the new Iraqi police or army forces, or those trying to form a new government— would become the victims of suicide bombers. The plan was brutally effective. More than 2,500 American service people have been killed in Iraq, during the invasion and in the insurgency that followed. Many thousands of

Iraqis have been murdered. In April 2006 alone, more than a thousand Iraqis were murdered in Baghdad by bombings or other criminal acts.

The suicide bombing attacks have not been limited to military targets but have also included mosques, Red Cross offices and installations, and private homes. As the war-torn country struggles to create a government that will represent all the many Iraqi factions in the wake of Hussein's ouster, each round of elections is shadowed by the threat of bombings at polling stations. Several such incidents have occurred, but each time, the voters continued to come out in large numbers, and the country began fashioning a coalition government and democratic constitution. However, traditional ethnic tensions between Shiite and Sunni Muslims continue to grow—as have tit-for-tat suicide bombings and other violent attacks—threatening to plunge the country into an extremely bloody civil war.

Chechnya

In Asia, the Muslim people in Chechnya have been struggling to separate from Russian control since the collapse of the Soviet Union in the 1990s. The Chechen separatists fear being victimized by ethnic prejudice and prefer that their tiny region be left alone. Following World War II, Soviet dictator Joseph Stalin had the entire Chechen population relocated to Kazakhstan. Thousands of them died there before the Chechens were allowed to return to their homeland in the wake of Stalin's death in 1953.

In the post-Soviet era, some Chechens wished to remain loyal to Russia, while separatists began resorting to violent attacks to proclaim their desire for Chechen independence. While not every separatist faction has turned to violence, those that made that choice have proven deadly and quite effective. Several of the Chechen separatist groups have ties to Al Qaeda, and their tactics have become quite similar. As the struggle for freedom has grown fiercer with time, civilian targets have been included alongside military ones.

On December 27, 2002, there were twin suicide bombings in the Chechen capital, Grozny. These were among the deadlier of the suicide attacks in the country, leaving seventy-two dead and over five hundred injured. The suicide attacks did not end there but only escalated. The following May, a truck bomb took fifty-nine more lives and destroyed a government building. That month also saw the emergence of female suicide bombers, when two women killed themselves and sixteen others. In June 2003, another woman blew herself up on a bus, taking twenty civilian lives. Many Chechen women volunteer to become suicide bombers because they've lost loved ones to the struggle. They are often nicknamed Black Widows.

As summer 2003 wore on, Chechen attacks at a rock concert in Russia killed fourteen, followed by an August

Following the explosive and deadly conclusion to the Beslan school hostage situation on September 3, 2004, a fireman inspects the ruined gymnasium, searching for survivors.

bombing at a hospital that killed fifty. That December, another forty-four lives were taken when a train was blown apart. These attacks continued through 2004 and 2005 with rising death tolls on both sides. The most noteworthy attack during that time was a suicide bombing of an airplane by two women, resulting in the deaths of ninety people.

The most violent, deadly, and tragic of all Chechen terrorist attacks occurred between September 1 and 3, 2004. On the first day of school at an elementary school in Beslan, Russia, thirty-two Chechen terrorists (male and female) stormed the building and took more than a thousand teachers, children, and their parents hostage. The terrorists quickly strung explosives throughout the building and wired them to go off if the school was stormed by security forces. As a condition for the release of the hostages, they demanded the withdrawal of all Russian troops from Chechnya.

After a three-day standoff with local police and Russian army forces, gunfire erupted and—either accidentally or intentionally—some of the bombs exploded. The police and armed forces went in, and a chaos of shooting and explosions ensued. When it was all over, 344 civilians were killed, including 186 children. Hundreds were wounded. Only one of the terrorists survived and later pleaded guilty to charges of murder, terrorism, and kidnapping.

Sri Lanka

Though far from the Middle East, suicide bombings have also proven to be an effective tool on the island of Sri Lanka in the Indian Ocean. The island's ethnic strife and civil war have not received as much international coverage as similar conflicts elsewhere, but they have been no less deadly.

In fact, the Black Tiger unit of the terrorist rebel group the Tamil Tigers began using the tactic on July 5,

1987. Since then, it has recorded more than 150 attacks, using more than 240 bombers. The Tigers have claimed the lives of many noteworthy political figures from India and Sri Lanka. For example, one Tamil Tiger, Thenmuli Rajaratnam, assassinated former Indian prime minister Rajiv Gandhi in a suicide bomb attack in May 1991.

The conflict on the island is more than a century old and was created in part by English colonists who intentionally ignited tensions between the island's ethnic groups—Sinhalese, Tamils, Muslims, and Burghers—in order to create a disorder that only they could control. This ensured their continued role in the island's governing. After the English eventually gave up control of the island in 1947, Sri Lankans were left with growing resentments that turned into an all-out struggle for land and power among the various ethnic groups.

From out of this conflict arose the Liberation Tigers of Tamil Eelam (LTTE), who want to create a separate Tamil-speaking country in the northeast of Sri Lanka called Tamil Eelam. Since its founding, the LTTE has taken control of land and managed its seized territories as a quasi-government, even though it is not officially recognized as a legitimate, independent governing body or political party by any of the world's nations. Instead, the international community has routinely condemned the Tigers' harsh and violent actions in their quest for independence. Many have gone so far as to equate the organization with Hezbollah and Hamas.

The Tigers have earned their reputation as terrorists for the way they fight to the death, indoctrinating their soldiers from the beginning that sacrifice is expected of them. This includes, when necessary, the ultimate sacrifice of suicide. Each soldier carries with him a cyanide capsule. If captured, he must take this deadly poison that will instantly kill him. The Black Tigers also carry out suicide bombing missions, such as the January 5, 1988, attack in which a truck filled with explosives was driven into the Sri Dalada Maligawa (Temple of the Tooth), considered to be one of the most sacred Buddhist temples in the world.

Another shocking attack occurred on May 14, 1998, when a Black Tiger stepped in front of a vehicle containing Sri Lankan brigadier Larry Wijeratne. The Tiger was wearing explosives and detonated himself, killing the brigadier. The largest recorded Black Tiger mission was the July 24, 2001, attack at Bandaranaike International Airport. Fourteen men entered the airport grounds in three waves. Once reaching the runway and hangars, they used antitank guns, grenade launchers, machine guns, and explosives to destroy or damage twenty-six aircraft. The Tigers also killed six airmen before being killed themselves.

The Tamil Tigers include a woman's branch, called Suthanthirap Paravaikal (Freedom Birds). One of these

Armed members of the Liberation Tigers of Tamil Eelam (LTTE) pose with their rifles at a Tamil base in eastern Sri Lanka in March 2004. The Tamil Tigers accept both men and women as militia members.

women detonated a suicide bomb at a political rally in Colombo, on December 18, 1999. She may have been trying to assassinate Sri Lankan president Chandrika Kumaratunga. He was not seriously injured, but ten Sri Lankans were killed and three others were hurt.

Despite a Norwegian-negotiated cease-fire that was put into effect in 2001, the Tamil Tigers have committed over 3,100 violations of the agreement, including the suicide bombing that killed Major General Parami Kulatunga, one of Sri Lanka's highest-ranking army generals, in June 2006.

Suicide or Martyrdom?

A debate among religious scholars and clerics has raged through the current cycle of suicide bombings. At issue is whether or not the suicide attacks are sinful and pro-hibited by Islamic law or are considered martyrdom, which represents a step toward paradise.

Many religious scholars and Muslim clerics insist that suicide is clearly forbidden in Islam. However, the Koran also indicates that fighting for the Islamic cause will absolve a person of sin and reserve him or her a place in paradise. In Saudi Arabia, Sheikh Abdul Aziz bin Abdullah al-Sheikh issued a religious edict, known as a fatwa, which clearly linked bombings with suicide, making the acts a sin. The fatwa was countered by Mohammed Sayed Tantawi, a respected theologian among Sunni Muslims. He wrote for *Al Ahram*, an Egyptian publica-tion, "If a person blows himself up, as in operations that Palestinian youths carry out against those they are fighting, then he is a martyr. But if he explodes himself among babies or women or old people who are not fighting the war, then he is not considered a martyr."

Other Suicide Bombings Around the World

Suicide bombers are not unique to certain regions of the world, nor are they all associated with organizations seeking certain political or religious goals. It is important to note that not all suicide bombers are Islamist radicals. Terrorism expert Robert Pape was quoted in March 2006 as saying, "Fifty percent of suicide attacks are not affiliated with Islamic terrorism." Suicide bombers have operated all over the world and have represented a wide range of causes and religions. Between 2000 and 2003, the world witnessed 312 suicide attacks, claiming 5,354 lives.

Ireland

For most of the twentieth century, the Irish Republican Army (IRA) sought to drive British troops out of the six counties of Northern Ireland. In the 1990s, they forced some of their members to become suicide bombers. Threatening their families with death, the IRA blackmailed men to drive bomb-laden trucks onto British army or Royal Ulster Constabulary bases (the constabulary is the region's police force). The group abandoned this tactic after widespread public outrage and protest.

Bali

In October 2002, five men in Bali formed a suicide pact and blew themselves up at the popular nightspots Paddy's and the Sari Club, killing over two hundred people and causing panic. It was later established that the funding for this attack came from Al Qaeda. Indonesia, which

A car bomb explosion on October 12, 2002, resulted in this fire in a popular nightclub in the Kuta Beach area of Bali, Indonesia. More than 180 people were killed in the bombing and subsequent fire.

contains a very large Muslim population, is the first Southeast Asian country to be targeted by Islamist radicals, and terror attacks have occurred there every year since 2001.

England

In a highly coordinated attack on July 7, 2005, Al Qaeda signaled its displeasure with England's participation in the 2003 U.S.-led invasion of Iraq by setting off suicide bombs on a London bus and in the subway system. Three bombs exploded at various points in the Underground

Four of the suspects in the July 7, 2005, London suicide bombings of Underground trains and a city bus appear in this surveillance video entering a train station on the morning of the attacks.

system within fifty seconds of each other, while the bus bombing occurred about an hour later. In addition to the four bombers, fifty-six people were killed, and seven hundred were injured.

Turkey

The Kurdistan Workers' Party wants to create a separate Kurdish state in what is currently southeastern Turkey. Known as the PKK (Partiya Karkeren Kurdistan), the group rose to prominence in the 1980s by using the familiar tactics of terrorism, including suicide bombings. It attacked military and civilian targets and has been known to strike civilians who refuse to aid the PKK. Suicide bombers have been called "strategic assets" by the PKK in its ongoing struggle. It is also the only terror organization known to have killed a member for refusing to become a suicide bomber.

The Recruiting and Training of Suicide Bombers

The conventional thinking is that people who choose to become suicide bombers do so because they are poor, uneducated, desperate, lack opportunities, and feel they have nothing to lose. Given the increasing number of attacks over the last twenty-five years, a more accurate profile has been constructed. Surprisingly, the typical suicide bomber is actually a middle-class, well-educated male in his twenties. He usually has given up his lucrative career, and sometimes his family, to answer a spiritual calling.

Some public policy experts argue that a country's level of terrorist violence is directly connected to its level of political freedom. The less political freedom—the less ability to express oneself politically and participate in decision making—the higher the likelihood of terrorist attacks.

Surprisingly, the typical suicide bomber is actually a middle-class, well-educated male in his twenties. He usually has given up his lucrative career, and sometimes his family, to answer a spiritual calling.

"A suicide attacker could be anyone," terrorist expert Daniel Benjamin told the *New York Times*. "He doesn't have to be trained, just indoctrinated. There's no profile; that's what makes it so hard to defend against." People have attempted to profile the bombers, however, and one Israeli study of Palestinian suicide bombers indicated that:

- Forty-seven percent of the suicide bombers have an academic education, and an additional 29 percent have at least a high school education.
- Eighty-three percent of the suicide bombers are single.
- Sixty-four percent of the suicide bombers are between the ages of eighteen and twenty-three; most of the rest are under thirty.
- Sixty-eight percent of Palestinian suicide bombers have come from the Gaza Strip.

There's no question that a certain frame of mind is essential to undertake the role of suicide bomber. The cable news channel MSNBC spoke with representatives of Hamas, investigating the level of mental preparation the bombers go through for months in advance of their mission. The unnamed Hamas official said, "The bombers believe they are sent on their missions by God, and by the time they're ready to be strapped with explosives, they have reached a hypnotic state. Their rationale: that by blowing themselves up in a crowd of Israelis, they are forging their own gateway to heaven" (as quoted in Ellis Shuman's article "What Makes Suicide Bombers Tick?").

Thousands of Muslim men offer Friday prayers at a mosque in Baghdad, Iraq, in 2003. Some mosques are believed to be centers of terrorist recruiting efforts.

Reports on Britain's BBC network indicate that suicide bomber recruits are drawn from those Muslims who demonstrate exceptional religious fervor. These recruits are "picked out from mosques, schools, and religious institutions. They are likely to have shown particular dedication to the principles of Islam . . . and are taught the rewards that will await them if they sacrifice their lives."

Yet not all suicide bombers are motivated primarily by religion. Some are driven more by political passion, rage, or concern for family. In her book *Growing Up Palestinian*, Laetitia Bucaille explains how Israeli occupation of lands Palestinians believe belong to them has allowed violent resentment and hostility to flourish.

The series of suicide attacks against Israeli civilians that began in 1994 had caused [a] hardening of attitudes. The loss of freedom of movement directly affected most of the [Palestinian] population . . . Faced with the constraints of the occupation, which smother every form of social, economic, or personal aspiration, Palestinian youth are caught between the impossibility of living under such circumstances and the dream of effacing the exile of their kin. It seems to them absolutely necessary to send in more and more suicide bombers, if Palestine is ever to be liberated. All of the volunteers who blow themselves up in the heart of Israel's cities are recruited from a group between eighteen and twenty-four years old.

Mouin Rabbani, director of the Palestinian American Research Center, points out that a very real, personal passion motivates these youthful suicide bombers. They are not necessarily brainwashed or blinded by religious faith. "Religious or ideological fervor appears to offer only a partial explanation. Palestinian suicide bombers are neither products of a passive and unquestioning obedience to political authority nor pressed into service against their will."

Additionally, some bombers sacrifice themselves in order to help their families or achieve glory. A *London Daily Telegraph* report said, "Lured by promises of financial stability for their families, eternal martyrdom and unlimited sex in the afterlife, dozens of militant Palestinians . . . aspire to blow themselves up, Israeli and Palestinian officials say. Their goal: to kill or injure as many Jews as possible in the hope that Israel will withdraw from Gaza and the West Bank."

Recruiting Children

The BBC also reported in 2001 that the terrorist group Islamic Jihad had organized a terror school to indoctrinate teenagers. Given its continuing holy war, or jihad, with Israel, the group needed to build its ranks. The youths, having grown up amid violence, were seen as especially susceptible to the appeal of terror. "We are teaching the children that suicide bombing is the only thing that makes the Israeli people very frightened. Furthermore, we are teaching them that we have the right to do it," one of the instructors, Mohammed el Hattab, told the network.

Palestinian boys throw rocks at an Israeli tank in the West Bank city of Hebron in January 2003. The Israelis were sweeping the area, seeking out Palestinian militants.

As part of the classes, the students drew pictures of Israeli victims of suicide attacks or self-portraits depicting themselves as armed and ready to give their lives for the cause. In exchange for successfully completing a suicide attack, the teens are told they will become martyrs, their spirits traveling to paradise where they will be greeted by seventy-two virgins. In fact, the guarantee of heaven and waiting virgins is a common recruiting tactic pitched to the faithful of all ages.

In an article on these terrorist-supported schools, *London Daily Telegraph* noted, "In Hamas-run kindergartens, signs on the walls read: 'The children of the kindergarten are the *shaheeds* (holy martyrs) of tomorrow.' The classroom signs at Al-Najah University in the West Bank and at Gaza's Islamic University say, 'Israel has nuclear bombs, we have human bombs.'" Hamas has taken to creating Web sites for children, urging them to become suicide attackers when they come of age.

Palestinian boys listen to the teachings of a Muslim cleric in this Hamas-funded summer school in July 2006.

Yousef Aref, a teacher in Nablus, told the *Christian Science Monitor*, "Nobody is recruited by force—they come voluntarily. They don't recruit teenagers. But young teenagers are motivated and want to be recruited, so they put pressure on the older ones to recruit them." That particular report noted the guidelines for recruits excluded anyone under twenty, an only son, or a young man who has lost his brother.

Recruiting children is not limited to the Middle East. Amnesty International reported in early 2006 that the LTTE in Sri Lanka has continued to kidnap youths as young as twelve and train them as suicide terrorists. Two teens, who escaped LTTE captivity in March 2006, told of receiving strenuous training in weapons combat at the Trincomalee rebel camp and were told by their leaders to prepare to sacrifice their lives.

Female Suicide Bombers

Terrorism experts say 15 percent of suicide bombers worldwide are women. The first female bombers were members of Sri Lanka's Tamil Tigers, and they began their bombings in 1987. In recent years, a higher percentage of women have been involved in the Chechen attacks than in other terrorist attacks around the world.

Women have proven just as susceptible as men to the appeals made by the charismatic religious leaders who fan the flames of prejudice into a holy cause. One of the most powerful arguments made to attract women is that the bombing would not only prove their bravery and help the cause but would also show that they are equal to men, which is still an issue in some parts of the world. Religious leaders have also given women their blessing using a very loose interpretation of the Koran's teachings.

National Geographic examined female suicide bombers and reported that personal motivations drove women more than ideology.

The perception in the West is that these people are religious fanatics who don't care about life. In the stories we examined we found that not to be true. The families we talked to told us that their daughters weren't overly pious. Although they were very upset and distraught over occupation, they were normal girls.

In 2006, the online magazine *Slate* reported on the death of Ayat Akhras, a Palestinian woman, who set off a bomb inside an Israeli supermarket. Her death was seen as emblematic of the passion Palestinians of both sexes have for the destruction of Israel and the lengths to which they will go to bring it about. "She fit none of the standard descriptions of 'typical' suicide bombers," *Slate* reported. "Not only was she not male, she was not overtly religious, not estranged from her family, not openly associated with any radical groups. She can hardly be described as a woman without a future. She was young, she was a good student, and she was engaged to be married—all of which is why her death reveals a great deal about the changing nature of the Palestinian terror campaign."

A female Palestinian suicide bomber, Reem Salah Riashi, poses with an automatic rifle and the Koran before her January 14, 2004, suicide attack at the border between the Gaza Strip and Israel. A mother of two, Riashi killed herself and four Israelis.

The Training

Once people volunteer to become suicide bombers, they leave one world behind and enter another. *Time* magazine profiled an Iraqi man going by the alias Abu Qaqa al-Tamimi who operated a safe house for new recruits and provided intelligence and weapons to the terrorist operatives. He told *Time*, "Once a volunteer is placed in my care, I am responsible for everything in his life until the time comes for him to end it."

Beginning in September 2004, al-Tamimi began his work and within a year had organized thirty attacks. Some insurgent groups approached him with a specific target and an attack date, while others simply sought his tactical and logistical advice. Al-Tamimi stayed current on all information relating to targets, such as police stations or restaurants frequented by security forces.

Once the target and date were settled, the bombers were brought to al-Tamimi. They were then installed in a safe house and kept away from newspapers, radio, and television. Instead, they studied religious texts and listened to sacred music, keeping them focused on the "holiness" of their mission.

As the bombers prepared, al-Tamimi arranged for the explosives, fitting belts to the size of the men or making certain a car was in good enough shape to operate until it exploded. He would then refine his plans, constantly checking the target and the proposed timetable, ensuring nothing would be out of place. Occasionally, al-Tamimi would even walk the route himself to be certain of the plan's practicality. Then, satisfied the plan was sound, he would take the bombers to the spot, usually a few days in advance. This way they would become familiar with the surroundings, giving them confidence during the mission. He'd even show them alternate routes in case something unforeseen occurred and they had to improvise.

During the funeral of Hamas leader Abdel Rahman Hamad in October 2001, Hamas militants wear mock suicide belts. Hamad was killed by Israeli special forces, who assert that he was a terrorist mastermind.

In the hours prior to a mission, the bombers would make a video, saying farewell to their loved ones. These videos would usually be uploaded to Web sites, as grieving though proud families frequently like to show off the "good deeds" of their departed children following the suicide attack.

Time also profiled Iraqi suicide bomber trainee Marwan Abu Ubeida (an alias), who had trained for months before the scheduled completion of his mission. While awaiting his instructions, Ubeida prayed and read about other jihads throughout history. All of this was in keeping with the strict control the insurgents had over their "walking weapons."

Ubeida was twenty at the time and had already been a soldier for Al Qaeda in Iraq before volunteering to become a suicide bomber. It was six months before he was deemed to be trustworthy and granted permission to become a soldier. "It was the happiest day of my life," Ubeida told *Time*.

In the final days before his assignment, Ubeida would be kept in isolation, intensifying his prayers, fasting, and composing his farewell message. His final prayer, he said, would be, "First, I will ask Allah to bless my mission with a high rate of casualties among the Americans. Then I will ask him to purify my soul so I am fit to see him, and I will ask to see my mujahedin brothers who are already with him."

The Aftermath

Once a suicide bomber successfully completes the mission, his or her actions are celebrated. Video footage of the attack is quickly put on the Internet to boast of the success, glorify the martyr, and entice others to join the cause. Families receive professionally made portraits of their sacrificed loved ones, taken in the days leading up to the mission. They also get a copy of the farewell video.

Additionally, families usually receive financial support from the sponsoring terrorist organization, starting with the cost of the funeral and reception afterward. The families might also receive a monthly stipend ranging from $300 to $600, medical coverage, and education for any other children in the family—many of whom will in turn be recruited by the terrorist organization that is paying their bills.

Relatives of the Palestinian suicide bomber Samer Hammad watch his farewell video following his suicide attack on April 17, 2006. He killed nine people in Tel Aviv, Israel.

Families, including parents, siblings, and even spouses and children, often take pride in these suicide missions despite the loss of their loved ones. They even gain social status in their neighborhood, as if their lost relative was a movie star or big league athlete. The shock and sorrow of their loss is eased by being showered with praise, congratulations, food, gifts, and money.

Are Suicide Bombs Effective?

It has been estimated that suicide bombings are four times as likely to go off as planned as are other kinds of terror attacks. They are also less expensive and easier to plan and execute. As a result, insurgent groups around the world encourage people to volunteer for this ultimate act. However, the cycle of suicide bombings, which began in the early 1980s, has continued and escalated without any of the sponsoring organizations gaining their stated goals. At the time of this writing, Israel and Palestine remain at odds over territory and statehood, the coalition forces in Iraq continue to guide the country toward democracy, the Russians have not granted Chechens independence, and the Tamil region remains a part of Sri Lanka. It should be remembered, too, that kamikaze attacks did not help Japan stave off a crushing defeat in World War II.

Writing in the *Washington Times*, James Jay Carafano, a senior research fellow for defense and homeland security at the politically conservative Heritage Foundation, said:

Fact is, terrorists rarely win. True, they succeed at killing people—murdering innocents, destroying property, and creating misery—but that's not their intended goal. Terrorism by definition is violence with a political purpose. Terrorists are terrorists not by choice but by desperation. They

Russian soldiers load missiles onto a launcher in the Chechen Republic, part of the Russian Federation. The missiles are aimed at Chechen rebels who wish to separate from Russia and establish an independent Islamic state.

kill men, women, and children indiscriminately because they think there's no other way to advance their cause. Propaganda and politics have failed them. They lack armies or economic power. There have been many terrorist campaigns throughout history. But most have failed to achieve their goals. Slaughtering civilians rarely advances political causes.

In fact, many times the offended country strikes back. Israel routinely retaliates swiftly and devastatingly, with the Israeli Defense Force usually demolishing homes that belong to families whose children volunteered for suicide bombing runs. Israel has even launched targeted assassination missions, killing leading terrorist masterminds in the occupied territories. Russian reprisals against Chechen attacks have been brutal. America saw to it that the Taliban was toppled in Afghanistan, dealing a major blow to Al Qaeda operations.

The Israeli-Palestinian conflict has demonstrated that, despite the various accords agreed to by Israeli and Palestinian politicians, considerable sections of both populations have objected, and Palestinian terrorists have stepped up the number of attacks. This in turn leads to public pressure in Israel for harsh counterattacks, which the Israeli army generally carries out. In an attempt to prevent further suicide bombings and other armed attacks, Israel began to construct a fence dividing Israeli and Palestinian lands. Such acts have certainly influenced both sides—at the negotiating table and in the voting booth—as witnessed by Hamas's surprise win in the January 2006 election over Fatah, the party of the late Yasir Arafat and longtime official representative of the Palestinian people.

A Palestinian woman holds balloons and celebrates the Hamas victory in Palestinian parliamentary elections held in January 2006.

Additionally, suicide bombers have caused internal conflict within populations. For example, in February 2006, ethnic disputes within Iraq led to the outbreak of suicide attacks as Iraqi targeted Iraqi, threatening to plunge the country into civil war. Scholars and clerics continued fiercely to debate whether these missions were acts of suicide—forbidden by Islam—or the acts of martyrs, who would be welcomed into paradise as a result of their deeds.

Yet support for this style of attack remains high among the populations from which the bombers are recruited. Dr. Nabil Kukali and the Palestinian Center for Public Opinion conducted a survey that showed 76.1 percent of the Palestinian population supported suicide attacks, 12.5 percent opposed them, while 11.4 percent had no opinion.

Terrorist leaders seem to have the patience to kill a few people at a time, score minor "victories," and gradually wear their enemies down. And as the enemy gets worn down, there seems never to be a shortage of volunteers for suicide bombing missions.

What people in the West do not fully grasp is that leaders like Osama bin Laden see their struggles as long-term objectives and know their ultimate goal may take centuries to achieve. They seem to have the patience to kill a few people at a time, score minor "victories," and gradually wear their enemies down. And as the enemy gets worn down, there seems never to be a shortage of volunteers for suicide bombing missions. Whether to ensure care and financial stability for their family, to gain personal glory, or to rise to a promised paradise, men and women continue to sign up for, train for, and commit acts of terror, paid for with their own lives.

Glossary

Allah Allah is the Arabic name for God; it translates as "the One."

fatwa In Islam, a declarative legal interpretation by a cleric or religious jurist that has been used for a range of purposes, from influencing court decisions to justifying terrorist activities.

fundamentalism Strict adherence to original doctrines and texts (usually religious), allowing for no alternative interpretations.

Gaza Strip The densely populated region along the Mediterranean coast that Israel took from Egypt during the 1967 Six Days' War and continues to occupy.

insurgent A person who participates in an organized rebellion against a military or governmental authority using a specific set of military tactics. These tactics tend to be more covert (including terrorist attacks) than outright armed conflict.

Islam Arabic word for "submission," but now used to describe a religious belief system in which a follower submits to Allah and acknowledges Muhammad as Allah's chief prophet.

jihad An Arabic word for "holy war." The importance of jihad is key to Muslims who follow the Koran and teachings of Muhammad, yet there is great disagreement over exactly who is to be fought and how. Many believe that a true jihad is directed against the rulers of an unjust regime, not against the people who are ruled by it.

Koran Arabic word for "recitation," it is also the name of Islam's holy book. Allah is said to have revealed the book to Muhammad over the course of his life while in Mecca or Medina. Under a subsequent leader, the caliph Uthman, the various pieces were finally collected in a single volume.

mujahedin Arabic for "one who practices jihad." First used to describe the Muslim warriors who fought against the Soviet Union's invasion of Afghanistan in the late 1970s and 1980s.

Muslim A believer in Islam.

Shiite A branch of the Muslim religion (also known as Shia), centered in Iran, with large followings in southern Iraq, Syria, and Lebanon. Shiites, numbering 10 percent of Muslims worldwide, believe Ali was the only true caliph (spiritual leader).

Sunni The largest Muslim sect, with 90 percent of the world's Muslim followers; they accept the first four followers of Muhammad as true caliphs.

terrorism Violence designed to create an atmosphere of fear and alarm among soldiers and civilians. All terrorist acts are crimes. They are committed to force a particular desired outcome.

For More Information

Central Intelligence Agency (CIA)
Office of Public Affairs
Washington, DC 20505
(703) 482-0623
Web site: https://www.cia.gov

Council on Foreign Relations
Washington Office
1779 Massachusetts Avenue NW
Washington, DC 20036
(202) 518-3400
Web site: http://www.cfr.org/index.html

Department of Homeland Security (DHS)
Washington, DC 20528
(202) 282-8000
Web site: http://www.dhs.gov/dhspublic

Federal Bureau of Investigation (FBI)
J. Edgar Hoover Building
935 Pennsylvania Avenue NW
Washington, DC 20535-0001
(202) 324-3000
Web site: http://www.fbi.gov

United Nations
First Avenue at 46th Street
New York, NY 10017
(212) 754-7098
Web site: http://www.un.org

U.S. Department of Justice
950 Pennsylvania Avenue NW
Washington, DC 20530-0001
Web site: http://www.usdoj.gov

U.S. Department of State
2201 C Street NW
Washington, DC 20520
(202) 647-4000
(800) 877-8339
Web Site: http://www.state.gov

Web Sites

Due to the changing nature of Internet links, Rosen Publishing has developed an online list of Web sites related to the subject of this book. This site is updated regularly. Please use this link to access the list:

http://www.rosenlinks.com/in/subo

For Further Reading

Bergen, Peter. *Holy War, Inc.: Inside the Secret World of Osama bin Laden.* New York, NY: Free Press, 2002.

Bloom, Mia. *Dying to Kill: The Allure of Suicide Terror.* New York, NY: Columbia University Press, 2005.

Fridell, Ron. *Terrorism: Political Violence at Home and Abroad.* Berkeley Heights, NJ: Enslow Publishers, 2001.

Friedman, Lauri S., ed. *What Motivates Suicide Bombers?* Farmington Hills, MI: Greenhaven Press, 2004.

Gambetta, Diego, ed. *Making Sense of Suicide Missions.* New York, NY: Oxford University Press, 2005.

Landau, Elaine. *Suicide Bombers: Foot Soldiers of the Terrorist Movement.* New York, NY: Twenty-first Century Books, 2006.

Miller, Debra A. *Suicide Bombers.* San Diego, CA: Lucent Books, 2006.

Pape, Robert. *Dying to Win: The Strategic Logic of Suicide Terrorism.* New York, NY: Random House, 2005.

Ruschmann, Paul. *The War on Terror.* New York, NY: Chelsea House Publications, 2005.

Victor, Barbara. *Army of Roses: Inside the World of Palestinian Women Suicide Bombers.* New York, NY: Rodale Press, 2003.

Bibliography

Applebaum, Anne. "Girl Suicide Bombers." Slate. April 2,
    2002. Retrieved February 2006 (http://www.slate.com/
    ?id=2063954).

Bergen, Peter. *Holy War, Inc.: Inside the Secret World of
    Osama bin Laden*. New York, NY: Free Press, 2002.

Bloom, Mia. *Dying to Kill: The Allure of Suicide Terror*.
    New York, NY: Columbia University Press, 2005.

Bucaille, Laetitia. *Growing Up Palestinian*. Princeton, NJ:
    Princeton University Press, 2004.

Carafano, James Jay. "Terrorist Theory of Victory."
    Washington Times, July 24, 2005.

Chehab, Zaki. *Inside the Resistance*. New York, NY:
    Nation Books, 2005.

Cooke, Jeremy. "School Trains Suicide Bombers." BBC
    News. July 18, 2001. Retrieved February 2006 (http://
    news.bbc.co.uk/1/hi/world/middle_east/1446003.stm).

Ghosh, Aparisim. "Inside the Mind of an Iraqi Suicide
    Bomber." *Time*, July 4, 2005.

Ghosh, Aparisim. "Professor of Death." *Time*,
    October 24, 2005.

Handwerk, Brian. "Female Suicide Bombers: Dying
    to Kill." National Geographic. December 13,
    2004. Retrieved February 2006 (http://news.

nationalgeographic.com/news/2004/12/1213_041213_
tv_suicide_bombers.html).

Jehl, Douglas. "Experts Fear Suicide Bomb Is Spreading
West." *New York Times*, July 13, 2005.

Kher, Unmesh. "Suicide Strategy." *Time*, July 4, 2005.

Margalit, Avishai. "The Suicide Bombers." *New York
Review of Books*, January 16, 2003.

"Now Assassins Queue Eagerly for Martyrdom." *London
Daily Telegraph*, September 13, 2001.

Nunan, Patricia. "Southeast Asia Suicide Bombers."
GlobalSecurity.org. November 27, 2002. Retrieved
February 2006 (http://www.globalsecurity.org/security/
library/news/2002/11/sec-021127-245ea765.htm).

Oliver, Anne Marie, and Paul F. Steinberg. *The Road to
Martyr's Square: A Journey into the World of the
Suicide Bomber*. New York, NY: Oxford University
Press, 2005.

Pape, Robert. *Dying to Win: The Strategic Logic
of Suicide Terrorism*. New York, NY: Random
House, 2005.

Prusher, Ilene R. "As Life Looks Bleaker, Suicide
Bombers Get Younger." *Christian Science Monitor*,
March 5, 2004.

Reuter, Christoph. *My Life Is a Weapon: A Modern
History of Suicide Bombing*. Princeton, NJ: Princeton
University Press, 2004.

Schweitzer, Yoram. "Suicide Terrorism: Historical Back-ground and Risks for the Future." PBS.org. June 18, 2004. Retrieved February 2006 (http://www.pbs.org/wnet/wideangle/shows/suicide).

Shuman, Ellis. "What Makes Suicide Bombers Tick?" *IsraelInsider*, June 4, 2001. Retrieved February 2006 (http://www.israelinsider.com/channels/security/articles/sec_0049.htm).

"Suicide Attack." Wikipedia. Retrieved February 2006 (http://en.wikipedia.org/wiki/Suicide_bomber).

"Suicide Bombers: Why Do They Do It, and What Does Islam Say About Their Actions?" About.com. Retrieved February 2006 (http://islam.about.com/cs/currentevents/a/suicide_bomb.htm).

Tanaka, Yuki. "Japan's Kamikaze Pilots and Contemporary Suicide Bombers: War and Terror." *Japan Focus*, November 25, 2005. Retrieved February 2006 (http://www.japanfocus.org/article.asp?id=458).

Van Biema, David. "Why the Bombers Keep Coming." *Time*, December 17, 2001.

Victor, Barbara. *Army of Roses: Inside the World of Palestinian Women Suicide Bombers*. New York, NY: Rodale Press, 2003.

Index

About the Author

Robert Greenberger is a New York–based writer who works for a national weekly newspaper. He has written books on a wide range of historical, political, and current events topics, in addition to several biographies of prominent world figures. He graduated from Binghamton University with a degree in both history and English.

Photo Credits

Cover (top) © Christopher Furlong/Getty Images; cover (middle) © Saif Dahlah/ AFP/Getty Images; cover (bottom left) © Ali al-Saadi/AFP/Getty Images; cover (bottom right), p. 25 © Wathiq Khuzaie/Getty Images; pp. 3 (left), 35 © Per Wilkund/ Corbis; pp. 3 (right), 47 © David Silverman/Getty Images; p. 4 (top) © Peter Macdiarmid/Getty Images; pp. 4 (middle), 12 (middle) © AFP/Getty Images; p. 4 (bottom) © Muhannad Fala'ah/Getty Images; pp. 5, 20 (bottom) © Karim Sahib/ Getty Images; p. 7 © STF/AFP/Getty Images; p. 8 © Bettmann/Corbis; p. 11 © Keystone/Getty Images; pp. 12 (top), 50 (top) © Mahmud Hams/AFP/Getty Images; p. 12 (bottom) © Philippe Bouchon/AFP/Getty Images; p. 14 © AP/Wide World Photos; p. 16 © Hans Pinn/GPO/Getty Images; p. 17 © Said Khatib/AFP/Getty Images; pp. 18, 37 (top, bottom) © Abid Katib/Getty Images; p. 20 (top) © Lakruwan Wanniarachchi/AFP/Getty Images; p. 20 (middle) © Qassem Zein/AFP/ Getty Images; p. 22 © CNN/Getty Images; p. 28 © Mikhail Klimentiev/AFP/Getty Images; p. 32 © Sena Vidangama/AFP/Getty Images; p. 36 © Metropolitan Police Handout/AFP/Getty Images; p. 37 (middle) © Awad Awad/AFP/Getty Images; p. 39 © Mario Tama/Getty Images; pp. 42, 45 © Getty Images; p. 43 © Thomas Coex/ AFP/Getty Images; p. 49 © Jaafar Ashtiyeh/AFP/Getty Images; pp. 50 (middle, bottom), 51 © EPA/AFP/Getty Images; p. 53 © Mohammed Abed/AFP/Getty Images.

Designer: Tom Forget; Photo Researcher: Amy Feinberg